Taking the Initiative and Value Addition

Virender Kapoor

Qurate
qouratebooks.com

TAKING THE INITIATIVE AND VALUE ADDITION
Virender Kapoor

Published by Qurate Books Pvt. Ltd.

Published in 2023

ISBN: 978-81-96261-85-6

Qurate Books Pvt. Ltd.
Goa 403523,
India www.quratebooks.com
Tel: 1800-210-6527, Email: info@quratebooks.com

Contents

1. What is Initiative and Value Addition? 7
2. What does It entail? 12
3. Some Basic Tips to Act Upon 17
4. Tech Giants 22
5. How Institutions are Built by Great Men 33
6. Great Companies 48
7. What Your Zodiac Sign Says for you 60

Self-Assessment Questions Taking the Initiative and Value Addition 69

Taking the Initiative and Value Addition

"Journey of a thousand miles starts with the first step".

Initiative is a quality that differentiates a leader from a follower. A leader moves first, and urges others also to move, whereas a follower waits for the leader to push him. Leaders also do what is not usually done-out of the box. Also do more than what you are asked to do- that extra mile is called value addition. This book teaches you both

1

What is Initiative and Value Addition?

A S THE Y S AY, "THE journey of a thousand miles starts with the first step." How true it is—unless you lift up your foot and take a step, how do you proceed further? This is true for everything—even for a job or assignment that we need to accomplish. It is a quality that often differentiates a leader from a follower. A leader moves first, takes the first step, and urges others also to move, whereas a follower waits for the leader to either push him or pull him along. Some people have God's gift of being in the front and taking the lead wherever they go—they always show the way and take people along on the journey. Others always remain in the confines of their comfort zone, never move on their own, and have to be told or pushed even to follow the herd.

To school children, initiative means doing something without being told to do so. A step further for them would be doing something that others either fail to do or do not attempt to do at all. Initiating something is what leadership is all about. The word leader means a person who leads, who is in front, and who obviously takes the first step always. In schools, there are children who will take the initiative to start a small charity campaign for the poor. A group of children would be the first ones to think about it without the teacher telling them to do so. And that group may have a mastermind, "the initiator," who "thought" about it and "motivated" four or five of his friends, who further motivated the rest of the class. It matters as to whose idea it is.

Initiative always begins with a thought. A few boys in the college decide to organize a blood donation camp. It is the first thought that matters. Somebody says, "Why don't we organize a blood donation camp?" and that is the most important thing to say. After the thought takes shape with a concrete plan, people start doing value addition or adding value, contributing toward the success of the idea. For instance, once the blood donation camp is on, a group of students decides to take it further to nearby schools and colleges and ask for volunteers to join in. This suddenly makes the number of donors five times the expected number from their single college! This is a real value addition to the blood donation camp.

Now, the same boy who started the blood donation camp in the college becomes a successful manager eventually. He then asks a question, "Hey, why don't we start a group insurance scheme for our employees?"

He, thus, initiates an idea and then works toward its execution. Once the scheme is launched, another employee says, "Why don't we include the families also and give them the insurance cover? This way, we will be able to get a better deal and also do good for all the employees." This is a value addition to their initial plan.

Take a glass of clean water. Once you heat the water, it becomes a value addition.

Cluster of Initiative

There are some qualities that are related to initiatives and value addition. This is the cluster of related qualities:

Constructive, courageous, team player, quality conscious, proactive, volunteer, dedicated, visionary, accountable, energetic, assertive, innovator, enthusiastic, responsible, pathfinder, dynamic, motivated, bold and confident, decisive, perfectionist, risk-taker, trendsetter, captain, good learner, creative, intelligent, fast thinking, analytical, aiming high, value enhancer, contributor, craving for knowledge, farsighted, futuristic charismatic, go-getter, killer instinct, and spontaneous.

The secret to getting ahead is getting started. The secret of getting started is breaking your complex overwhelming tasks into small manageable tasks and then starting on the first one.

—Mark Twain

Being Proactive

Many times, people react and don't pro-act. Being proactive means taking action without anybody telling you to do it, or acting before a problem crops up. The trick to working better is to start acting before a problem starts, which means recognizing your responsibility to make certain things happen and being prepared to handle the problem before it becomes unmanageable. It is like being prepared all the time and seizing an opportunity before the opportunity seizes you.

Even if there is an existing problem, do we sit back and keep looking at the problem? Do we keep cursing the problem? Or do we get up and find a solution to that problem? You need to get hold of the problem first and shake it up before the problem gets hold of you and shakes you up instead. Proactive people create more proactive people and thereby create a proactive culture—a culture where people don't sit over problems but get up and take charge and get moving.

Therefore, think proactively, think of taking initiatives, and speak proactively and speak of taking initiatives. Instead of saying, "I may be able to do it," say, "I will be able to do it." Instead of saying, "There is nothing much I can do," say, "Let us see what all I can do."

Going That Extra Mile

Taking initiative is one thing and getting the job done is another thing.

Thereafter, doing a dash extra is what the ultimate test is for a go-getter.

Great people have the habit of, or even develop the habit of, doing that extra thing with gradual effort. Any fool can do what he is told to do.

Therefore, managers manage to do what is required to be done, whereas leaders do what is not usually done. They do the unusual— out-of-the-box thing—that extra zing, that extra topping, that unexpected act, that unanticipated thing, that out of the way thing, that offbeat thing. And they are the first ones to do it; that's why they are the initiators. These are the people bosses love; these are the people who get faster promotions.

Whenever I did performance appraisal of my team, I asked every individual, "Tell me what would not have happened in this organization had you not been a part of the organization?"

Everything you want is outside your comfort zone.

—Robert Allen

Beyond the Call of Duty

Now, I want to share a personal experience with you.

When I bought a house and moved in, I had no idea that the road in front of the house belonged to the housing society where we lived. Therefore, the maintenance of that road was not the responsibility of the municipal corporation. In a couple of weeks, I realized that the road was in a very bad condition and was told by the neighbors that for the last eight years, no maintenance was carried out there. The society was unable to muster enough funds for the road.

I spoke to a couple of neighbors and asked, "Why can't we get together and at least get it repaired or do up the part of the road which is in front of our plots?" People shrugged at my words first and thought that I was talking through my hat. I was dead serious about the idea and again spoke to a few guys. Gradually, people started believing in my "idea" and started thinking my way. We had a neighbor who had experience building roads but was leading a retired life. I roped him in and created a small core group and also a working group of another three neighbors. The ex-contractor gave us the estimated cost, and we divided it by the number of volunteers we had and arrived at a cost per house, which was a measly Rs. 5,000. I convinced them that they had spent millions of rupees in buying the property, then why couldn't they spend just Rs. 5,000 more to do value addition to their own property. I also told them that with a good road, their property value would further enhance and also fetch them better rentals. I was surprised at the response, and within a week, we had enough money to start the project!

The day I had initiated this idea, I had announced within the core group that I would ensure that we have a proper road by Diwali, which was only two months away at that time. But the way things moved, we could finish the road construction a week before Diwali, so I was exceptionally happy. We did experience hurdles, we did face some opposition from some people with a negative mindset—but we ultimately did it. We did it without any authority but with the cooperation of the people and the initiative that we took.

I feel our country would have developed a lot more, had we, as Indians, taken some more initiatives and been proactive by nature. From the road, we moved on to streetlights and then did some more beautification in the area. And then there was no looking back. Therefore, in a nutshell, you have to initiate an idea and thereafter work hard to get the project going. It can be done if you believe in it.

2

What does It entail?

Going Against the Flow

The easiest way to lead your life is by flowing along with the current of circumstances. Just go along with the flow, do nothing, and relax. Then you don't know where the flow will take you. That is exactly what will happen to you if you are in a river and allow the flow to drag you or push you as it pleases. You may hit a boulder, get into a whirlpool, but will never reach the river bank unless you struggle against the flow.

Similarly, if you want to succeed you must learn to go against the flow and work hard to go in the right direction.

The Story of Vardan Kabra

Vardan Kabra is an IIM-Alumnus—a person from a middle-class family who had also started to accomplish his necessities of money and power, like most of us, but later, realized his actual dream. He didn't even sit for the placements and he had also refused a very good pre-placement offer from Procter & Gamble (P&G), one of the reputed MNCs. Initially, his parents were not too happy with his decision because of the risk factor involved. But now, looking at his dedication, they fully support him and he is backed by his friends from the corporate sector who promised to join him soon.

He opened a school in Surat in 2005, and today, he has a school with more than two thousand students following the International Baccalaureate (IB) system of education. He started a school named The Fountainhead School, which is an ideal name for his school as it means the source of knowledge.

He says that his school will not only be focusing on academics but will stress on all-round development, and all students will be treated equally there. In designing his school's syllabus model, he got great support from a lady studying education psychology and curriculum development at the University of Georgia, who had written to him extending her help. He has also got inputs from a teacher in Australia, who wishes to share his ideas with him, and also from a person who develops education-related software. He has many other well-wishers who see their own dreams getting accomplished through his project. Remember, this is just the beginning; there is a lot more to come.

Thinking is easy, acting is difficult, and to put one's thoughts into action is the most difficult thing in the world.

—Johann Wolfgang Von Goethe

Beat Procrastination

The dictionary meaning of "procrastination" is to "defer action, especially without any good reason."

Many of us have a habit of delaying things, trying to defer things for the next day, or what we also call dilly-dallying. Most often, it is simple laziness, or at worst, a lack of motivation and lack of willpower to sustain that motivation to get going.

Okay, let us say you want to crack a competitive exam. What do you need to do for that?

You need to study regularly—say eight hours a day over a period of at least three months. Now, many would say, "Oh, I will start tomorrow," and that "tomorrow" will never come. Then, just a month before the exams, such people wake up and start studying frantically. These arethe people who willnever make it big in such exams. A winner will make sure that he has his aims and aspirations clearly set infront of his eyes and he will keep working hard from the day he decides to start his preparation. Then, what is the trick? There are afew things to beat procrastination—how not to defer action to achievethe desired results.

- **Avoid the process and think of the result:** If a 100-meters printer has to win a race or a gold medal, can he wait till thelast day to start practicing? No, he needs to prepare over a long period— even a year in advance—to achieve it. If he starts thinking— worrying about how cold it will be in the morning or how hot it will be during the summer or how much effort he will have to put in every day, then he may not be able to even start the practice sessions. In such a situation, one must look at the results or feeland imagine the results—that you are running the final race and you have actually won a medal. Now, that is what will motivate youto move on toward the goal.
- **Write down what you desire:** In this way, you describe your heart felt desire on paper: "Oh I must get into the best business school to do an MBA. I should get marketing as my specialization, and thereafter, get a job with a reputed company." Start imagining yourself in one of the IIMs or equivalent B-schools. This will motivate you. Unless you have a reasonable desire and you back it with good efforts, you can't win the race.
- **One bit at a time:** After your desire is clearly defined, it is time to get down to the execution. Here you must take it one step at a time.

Every day, write down one thing you can do that day, which will help you in achieving the results that you are seeking. On the first day, goand get relevant books from the library, get your writing material in order, organize your study table, and buy a table lamp.

So the line that you should have written for this, would be: "Today, I willget organized to start my studies from tomorrow." And once your table is set and you have all the books to read—you can begin your preparation from the next day. It's that simple!

- **How will each step help:** When you write a task for the day, also write how it will help you to achieve your over all goal. This gives you a boost to work every day.
- **Just do it:** After you have written the task for the day and its benefits, the nextstep is to just do it. Start the work once you have everything set, without any further delay.

'There comes a moment when you have to stop revving up the car and shove it into gear.'

—David Mahoney

Anticipation is the Key to Planning

Anticipating problems is the key to taking the initiative. Anticipation is like giving birth to an idea. I call this "mental gymnastics." A successful person always thinks ahead, plans ahead, and also prepares ahead oftime. Such a person keeps anticipating what is next. A good manager keeps track of his resources, keeps planning alternative strategies, and keeps monitoring the progress of his project at all times.

He always thinks ahead: "What will happen if two of my team mates fall sick? Do I have a few backup people? Can I bank on the human resource department for filling up the slots? Can I ask two more people from the team to undertake the additional responsibilities and work on the project overtime so that the project doesn't get delayed? Who would be the best two people for this task? Should I earmark bachelors in myteam for extra shifts at night?" So many questions have to be tackled—this is good management, which comes with experience. It isnot a pessimistic view—it is a practical way to handle day-to-day work more efficiently. This is being productive and not depending on others for anything. Why should you wait for a crisis to occur? Instead, you should plan for every crisis or anticipated problems or unfore seen circumstances way ahead of time.

Mental gymnasts try to see the unforeseen. This is mental initiative.

In the armed forces, contingency planning is an integral part of any plan. A general or a commander tries to anticipate the next move of the enemy. He looks at all the approaches from where the enemy forces can attack. It could be from the front, left, right, or even rarely through paradropping, or the enemy may attack by air in the day time. The very famous Pearl Harbor debacle happened because American generals could not anticipate an air attack from the aircraft carriers.

Their failure to anticipate led to the bloodshed.

An idea is worthless unless you use it.

—John Maxwell

3

Some Basic Tips to Act Upon

How to be Proactive on a Day-to-Day Basis

If you work more efficiently, you will be able to achieve much more, and you will enjoy your work. This is the simple reason for you notto ever get exasperated while doing your job. Many people who arenot proactive, and don't plan the day ahead, get exhausted and tiredduring the day's work. And that is why they lose enthusiasm to workthe next day.

Here are some tips:

- *Analyze your job*: Whenever you undertake an assignment or a job, you must first understand the job thoroughly—what is the routine work, what kind of problems can crop up during the day, what time of the day there is maximum work pressure, and several other similar issues.
- *Perform efficiently*: Plan in advance, create procedures, make check lists, instruct your team, get all the information needed in advance, train your people, and plan for all possible contingencies. At the end of the day, take feedback

to make the necessary changes for the next day. Learn from your mistakes and plan the next day to be much better.

- *Take preventive measures*: This is to stop problems from ever rising. Remember, "Prevention is better than cure" or "a stitch in time saves nine." When you are going for a long drive on a holiday, then itis wise to get your car serviced beforehand, ensure you have enough petrol, and make sure your spare tire has the standard pressure thatit is supposed to have, and the jack is in theboot.
- *Set priorities*: Everything is important, but everything is not equally important. Some points or jobs need to be cleared earlier than others. Therefore, the best method that I employ is to make a task table for the next day. Say there are fifteen jobs to be done. I write all of them in my diary. Thereafter, I prioritize them as P1, P2, and P3. The most important ones are marked as P1, and I attempt them first thing in the morning. Thereafter, I keep crossing the ones that have been done. All the points that have not been finished are carried forward to the next day. Whether you are the CEO of a company or a plumber, this method will fetch you rich dividends.
- *Avoid clutter*: Many times, we spend time attempting jobs thatare un important. They are the time wasters. These could be avoided or assigned to those who are not loaded with too manyimportant tasks.
- *Use technology*: Electronic calendars, reminders, mass mails, video conferencing, SMSes, etc., can be effectively used to enhance performance. Use computers for saving drafts of letters that are often repeated. It all depends on what sort of work you do—but technology can be an effective tool to stay ahead.
- *Sharpen your axe*: It is important to keep learning new techniques and brushing up the old ones. The world is moving fast, and in order to remain a head of others, you

must keep acquiring knowledge, education, and skills that will help you perform better and better. All the above are simple common sense, and if used regularly, can stop you from "fire fighting" every day. All the above also have an element of anticipation and initiative—you always expect the unexpected.

Give Solutions to Others

Whenever you work with people as a team leader, then your foremost job is to provide solutions and direction to the team.

People often provide direction but thereafter fail to provide the required solutions. Put yourself in your subordinate's shoes. If your boss doesn'tgive you any solution to your problems, what will you do? You may posea problem a few times over but there after, you will stop going to yourboss. You may then look for solutions elsewhere—say from your teammates, or in the worst case, you will have to approach the boss's boss! And then your boss will say, "You have by passed me," and thus, a wall will be built between the two of you, disrupting your ability to provide quality work.

So, the next time a subordinate comes to you, try to find a solution for his problem rather than turning a blind eye to it.

The Story of Super 30

Super 30—it sounds like a cricket tournament, something like Super 6 or 8. But no, what we are talking about is one of the greatest achievements made by two persons, who came up with an innovative idea and worked hard to get it in shape.

The two biggies behind Super 30 are Anand Kumar, a local mathematician, and Abhay Anand, a 1977 batch IPS officer, who iscurrently posted as inspector general, economic offences, with the Bihar government. Two years ago, while coaching his own children for the IIT entrance tests—both are IITians now—Abhayan and thought of the many underprivileged students who didn't have access to such facilities and yet many could make it with just a little help. That's when it occurred to him that he could start a tutorial for poor rural students.

To tap hidden talent from the rural areas of Bihar, he started The Ramanujan School in 2003. Anand, a topper in BSc physics, who was running a coaching center of his own, come forward to help him. Hed ecided to devote half his house at Mihanpur to this project and bear the entire expenses, which were about Rs. 1,000 per month per student.

All the facilities were provided to the students absolutely free there.

The Super 30 were meticulously selected after rigorous screening and several aptitude tests. It was a seven-month course and showed phenomenal results. Even today, they have retained the benchmark.

Two great people who felt and then undertook the responsibility to pay back to their community spend just a little free time of their own for a noble cause that is producing such wonders that even the most experienced tutors haven't been able to produce so far. This clearly signifies that God is with them, and proves that where there is a will, there is a way. This year, twenty-eight out of thirty students in their batch were selected for IIT. This success rate stands unparalleled.

The right man is the one who seizes the moment.

—Johann Wolf Gang Von Goethe

First-Mover Advantage

Remember the saying, "The early bird gets the worm"?

Take any walk of life, and you will realize that all those who got into the business first ended up making it big. People who set up factories first in rural areas were much more successful in times to come than those who came in later. Even in the telecom industry, the cellular service operators who come in first got the first-mover advantage and captured the market with millions of subscribers in their kitty. Those who moved in later had to struggle for a long, long time to make a mark with the subscribers.

In any field, the first-mover advantage is of great significance and is abig deciding factor for success. Those who move into a particular field first are the ones who are full of initiatives and thus are bound to havean upper hand in terms of advantages.

A good plan implemented today is better than a perfect planimplemented tomorrow.

—George Patton

The Essence

Initiative is basically as simple as taking the first step forward. School children, college students, working professionals, and top executives—all need to take initiative at some point inlife. This habit needs to bebuilt from our earlier days. Initiative begins with a thought—and this should then be followed by action. Being proactive is better than being reactive. Start working before a problem strikes. Therefore, think and speak proactively.

Procrastination is the biggest disease afflicting many people.

Such people always defer action and lack initiative.

They keep everything pending for the next day. They are actually "anti-initiative" people. This is because they lack motivation and willpower and are simply lazy. There are some simple ways of beating this lazy habit, which have been discussed in an earlier chapter. Anticipation and mental gymnastics are the key to remain ahead and be more productive. As managers and leaders, it is not enough to set a courseand an agenda; it is important to give solutions to problems when teammates get stuck somewhere.

You don't drown by falling in the water, you drown by staying there.

—Edwin Louis Cole

4
Tech Giants

THIS CHAPTER DETAILS four stories of young people who created history in the domain of technology.

Facebook

I think a simple rule of business is, if you do the things that are easier first, then you can actually make a lot of progress.

—Mark Zuckerberg

When in 2003, Mark Zuckerberg, a student at Harvard, thought of a small intranet for his fellow students to share their pictures, he could possibly never have realized what he was getting into. Nevertheless, he went on to implement it, and that was the first step to his becoming a billionaire. He did it; however, most that get an idea will not do it but drop it.

This innocent idea called Face Mash was to connect fellow students on a college network where they could not only load their pictures but could share other information, like their preferences, clubs, sports, class schedules, and hobbies. This was very much like college intranet networks controlled by the faculty to communicate about class schedules, holidays, assignments, reading material, etc. The only difference was that now it was student-driven and fun-filled. Since this flouted college norms, it had to be shut down in two days. Yet, within those forty-eight hours, four hundred and fifty students had joined this small community.

To circumvent the issue, Zuckerberg registered a company in February 2004 called The facebook.com. Very soon, students from Yale and Stanford joined the network, and within three months it had two hundred and fifty thousand students from more than thirty colleges! Was it a vision— a fluke vision—till then? Here the feeling must be *"yeh dill mange more,"* which was expansion and value addition. Then they opened the network for high school students and other universities too to join in, and by the end of 2004, they had a user base of one million!

Now you need to convert fluke into providence, and that's what Zuckerberg did. They tweaked the software to give more options and facilities to upload multiple pictures to reach out to a larger group of people by creating user walls and tagging facilities. Another value addition to the project at hand.

In 2005, highschool students and students at universities outside the United States were allowed to join the service. By year's end, it had six million monthly active users. It was like hitting a jackpot or stumbling upon a gold mine.

Conversations are happening whether you are there or not.

—Kim Garst

In 2006, Facebook opened its membership beyond students to anyone over the age of thirteen(teenagers), opening its flood gates to the world at large. This was the time to monetize their baby

Advertisers were able to create new and effective customer relationships. Initially household product manufacturer, Procter & Gamble attracted fourteen thousand people to a promotional effort by "expressing affinity" with a teeth-whitening product. This kind of direct consumer engagement on such a large scale had not been possible before Facebook, and more companies began using the social network for marketing and advertising.

They could never have imagined what could have been the driving force behind the mad rush of people joining this network.

If I have to do a post-success (not postmortem) analysis of Facebook's or any other platforms, like Twitter or WhatsApp, success, I feel the biggest driving force for a human being is the freedom to "express and reach out to people about what he feels about something."

That is why every sane constitution in a democratic setup has enshrined "freedom of speech and expression for every citizen" enshrined as a fundamental right.

Writing for an established newspaper is extremely difficult for an ordinary person, and the barriers are quite high. You may be lucky to have a letter to the editor published in some obscure corner of the paper, which may not even be read by anyone.

Social media platforms like Facebook allow instant feedback about what you said and what others feel. These are the methods of engagement. You can vent out your thoughts and feelings to people.

Suddenly, the rules of engagement hadchanged.

In today's world, expectations are so high—materialistically, personally, and politically—that even a sane person has gone crazy and become unhappy for no reason. Social media is that pressure cooker release mechanism, or what in psychological terms is called "catharsis" —venting out your feelings or vomiting out from your heart and brain. It is like mental *detox* to your heart's content.

A squirrel dying in front of your house may be more relevant to your interests right now than people dying in Africa.–

—Mark Zuckerberg

The flip side is that it is the "me too" feeling that is important for all humans and it is like self-actualization. Social media takes you to the fifth level of Maslow's hierarchy so easily and so quickly—free of cost—that you are bound to be a part of it.

BYJUS Teacher at heart: Byju Raveendran

We make a living by what we get, but we make a life by what we give.

—Winston Churchill

They say that teaching is a noble profession. Yes, it is. This is the only profession where your students/learners surpass you in every which way you can think off. Money, status, lifestyle, and more. But you get a great satisfaction that you have made a difference—you added value to the lives of the thousands you once taught. I have been teaching and grooming MBA students at Symbiosis for more than a decade, and I am proud of the fact that almost all of them are doing very well professionally—many have become CEOs, directors, and CTOs in prestigious companies in India and abroad.

Raveendran Byju was born and raised in a small town in the state of Kerala. His parents were teachers of math and science. He did engineering from the Government College of Engineering, Kannur, and joined a multinational shipping company as a service engineer.

He who serves the most reaps the most.

During his earned break from an overseas job as a service engineer in around 2003, Byju decided to help some of his friends appearing for the Common Admission Test (CAT) in Bangalore as he was good in math and science. It was a one-on-one yet informal, friendly way of teaching. He also took the exam to see how difficult it was to crack the most difficult competitive exam. The result was astounding; he had scored 100 percent! He was not sure whether it was a fluke. He again started teaching some of his friends, and took the test yet again in 2005, without any preparation, and scored a perfect 100 percent yet again. This time he also attempted IIM-A, B, and C interviews and cleared all of them. He did not opt for MBA.

Instead, he wanted to teach students how to crack CAT.

So, it was just by chance, that he took the entrepreneurial path, but teaching was a choice he made as he loved it. Gradually, through word of mouth, the number of students grew. Starting with two, it became four, then sixteen, and soon he would teach over a thousand students in an auditorium back in 2007. Demand was escalating, and he was hopping between ninecities to hold sessions, which were sold out beforehand, like he was a rock star holding a concert. "I was a teacher by choice and an entrepreneur by chance," says Raveendran.

We rise by lifting others.

—Robert Ingersoll

It was time to think out of the box if he wanted more people to benefit. Soon, with the help of some of his students who had graduated from IIMs, he started a company BYJU's. Now was the time to create a product that had reach as well as quality. Along with his former students, he started creating core learning products, and after four years of hard work and experimenting, they created these, which are today a part of the app-based format.

The idea was to create something that students could use easily. He says, "We ensured that the learning experience was created in a format that students preferred. It had to be effective, but we tried making it interesting with interactive videos. We are teaching students how they should learn rather than what they should learn. We focused on clearing fundamentals which is the root cause of not performing well in academics."

Once the product and market were ready, it was time to grow—and grow faster. By 2013, within two years, they got a funding of \$9 million. In 2015, another \$25 million camein and in 2016, \$125 million from two sources flowed in and by 2017, they signed up actor Shah Rukh Khan as brand ambassador. In 2017, they were valued at 600 million dollars and taken up as a case study in Harvard Business School. BYJU'sbecomes a billion-dollar company by the first quarter of 2018. By June 2020, it became the biggest ed-tech company in the world, with a valuation of $10.5 billion. This was followed by series of acquisitions, including Akaash educational services, for one billion dollars.

What a spectacular rise in just nineyears!

Giving is not just about making a donation. It is about making a difference.

—Kathy Calvin

Elon Musk: Initiative after initiative Tesla

The nation that leads the clean energy economy will be the nation that leads the global economy.

—Barack Obama

An avid reader, a diehard technologist with physics as his favorite subject, Elon Musk is a go-getter in the spirit of the word. He always wanted to do various things differently, and he did them. "Think big" is a lesson one can draw from his success journey.

He is a Bachelor of Science in Physics, as well as a Bachelor of Arts in Economics from the Wharton School. With a firm grip on technology and economics, these were a formidable combination for his dreams. Musk is a bookworm andhe reads voraciously—everything from encyclopedias to comic books.

His interest in science fiction, philosophy, and fantasy isreflected in his concern with human progress. He works in areas that he has identified as crucial to our future, specifically the internet, the transition to renewable energy sources, and space colonization.

The First Step

Musk started Zip2, a web software company, in 1995, which would help newspapers develop online city guides, and by 1999, Zip2 was acquired by Compaq's for a whopping $340 million. He was a key person in creating Pay Pal, from which he made $180 million in stocks. It was now his inner calling and passion for technology that drove him toward clean energy.

He did that and created an electriccar start-up called Tesla Motors.

The name Tesla was chosen in honor of Nikola Tesla, a Serbian American inventor, electrical engineer, mechanical engineer, and futurist, best known for his contributions to the design of the modern alternating current (AC) electricity supply system. Tesla experimented with mechanical oscillators, early X-ray imaging, and a wireless-controlled boat too. Well known as an inventor, he demonstrated his achievements to the rich and famous at his lab and was noted for his showmanship at public lectures.

Investing $70 million, he started his electric car venture and was hands-on in designing the Tesla Roadster. He then took over as the CEO and main product architect and designer. It became the most sought-after revolutionary car. It demonstrated Tesla's cutting-edge battery technology. Remember the biggest challenge in electric vehicles is a good, lasting battery, which is at the heart of it. This is where good research and development come into play.

Moving Forward

The company kept improving its product with constant value addition. and their first ever premium all-electric sedan—Model S—has become the best car in its class in every category, combining safety, performance, and efficiency.

With the longest range of any electric vehicle, regular software updates that keep updating and do a constant value addition, and a record 0–60 mph acceleration time of 2.28 seconds it is something out of the world. In 2017, Tesla began deliveries of Model 3, a mass-market electric vehicle with more than 320 miles of range, and unveiled Tesla Semi, which is designed to save owners at least $20,000 over 100,000 miles based on fuel costs alone. In 2019, Tesla unveiled Cybertruck, which has better utility than a traditional truck and more performance than a sports car, as well as the Model Y compact SUV, which began customer deliveries in early 2020.

In addition to producing electric vehicles for clean energy,

Tesla plays a major role in the solar energy space. Solar City, their clean energy-services company, produces two rechargeable solar batteries, mainly used for stationary energy storage purposes. The smaller Powerwall was developed for home backup power and off the-grid use, while the larger Power pack was designed for commercial or electric utility grid use. Tesla manufactures batteries at the volumes required to meet production goals while creating thousands of jobs.

Into Space Voyage

That's one small step for a man, one giant leap for mankind.

—Neil Armstrong

SpaceX

Musk deployed a substantial portion of the earnings of his PayPal sale to start Space Exploration Technologies Corporation, known as SpaceX, an interstellar travel company. Musk spent over $100 million to found SpaceX. It was founded in 2002 with the goal of reducing space transportation costs to enable the colonization of Mars. They have flown the Falcon 9 series of rockets over ahundred times.

SpaceX is also working on a satellite mega constellation named Starlink to provide commercial internet service. In January 2020, the Starlink constellation became the largest satellite constellation in the world.

With SpaceX, Musk landed several high-profile contracts with the National Aeronautics and Space Administration (NASA) and the US Air Force to design rockets and conduct military missions. Musk has been vocal about his plans to send an astronaut to Mars by 2025 in a collaborative effort with NASA.

In this single galaxy of ours there are eighty-seven thousand million suns.

—Arthur C. Clark

A Company that Needs no Introduction—Google

Research is seeing what everybody else has seen and thinking what nobody else has thought.

—Albert Szent-Györgyi

My first advice to anyone who enrolls in a PhD program is that he must start the project in a way that finally gives a strong starting point for writing a book. Are you doing a PhD for getting a stamped degree and calling yourself a doctor for life thereafter? Then your work (thesis) will keep gathering dust in some dingy archive room in the library, which possibly no one will ever look at again. My argument is simple. Is it worth spending four to five years of your life struggling with a topic to get a PhD that is of no use to anyone there after? Many scholars and professors in the west say that students enrolled for PhD don't really produce anything worth while. Does your work culminate into a book that enlightens ordinary men and women and enhances their knowledge a wee bit? Mostly, it doesn't.

Having said that, let me tell you that Google—around which the whole world revolves in a way goes and cannot really do without—was the trigger point from a PhD research project by Sergey Brin and Larry Page, both PhD students at Stanford University.

Google thus began in January 1996 in a dormitory in the college as a research project to make a search engine to look for information on the internet. This could have died anatural death in the dorm where it was conceived after they got their degrees unless something was done to take it further. Larry and Sergey took the initiative to make it better than other search engines.

While conventional search engines ranked results by counting how many times the search terms appeared on the page, they theorized about a better system that analyzed the relationships among websites. This was called the algorithm Page Rank; it determined a website's relevance by the number of pages and the importance of those pages that linked back to the original site. They nicknamed the new search engine Back Rub because the system checked back links to estimate the importance of a site.

In fact, the world needs more nerds.

—Ben Bernanke

What's in a Name?

This is an often-asked question. Today you have weird brand names like Ola, Oyo, Zomato, Uber, Dunzo, Pepperfry, Apple, Lacoste, Red Chillies, and hundreds like these.

Since Larry and Sergey were dealing with numbers, they looked at a word thatrepresented some huge figure and they hit upon a word that represented 1 followed by 100, which was googol.

Google sounded, better so they decided to call this product Google. The domain name, www.google.com, was registered on September 15, 1997. In August 1998, Sun cofounder Andy Bechtolsheim gave Larry and Sergey a cheque for $100,000, and Google Inc. was officially born.

Thereafter, there was no looking back, and two more angel investors chipped in.

VentureValue Addition

Now was the time to move forward and not be complacent with past laurels. They rapidly ramped up manpower and went full steam to create hundreds of products. Starting with search-related tools, they went onto Gmail, YouTube, advertisement tools, publishing and communication tools, map-related products, business tools, and even statistical tools.

Top-notch professionals want to work for them, and they have a workforce upward of 139,000.

Google generates most of its revenues from advertising. As of 2021, Google has an estimated net worth of around $420 billion. Alphabet, as a parent company to Google, has an estimated net worth of $900 billion, thus making it one of the most valuable companies in the world. Google makes an estimate of $50 million daily.

I would like to say they have added value to the alphabet "G" by creating, name, fame, and wealth of this order.

Research is formalized curiosity. It is poking and prying with a purpose.

—Zora Neale Hurston

5
How Institutions are Built by Great Men

THIS CHAPTER DEMONSTRATES how great educational institutes were built by one initiative taken by one good person. Here are five great stories to inspire you.

BITS Pilani

We don't get a chance to do that many things, and everyone should be really excellent. Because, this is our life.

—Steve Jobs

Institutes are built with the initiative of one person. It comes from the heart, and a seed is sown. It has to then be nurtured and grown to become a huge tree with branches, leaves, flowers, and fruits. All these branches, in the case of an institution, are like a graft, which is a value addition.

Birla Institute of Technology, popularly known as BITS, is a living example of such an institution.

It is located around 200 km from Delhi, as well as Jaipur, in a desert area, which is now like an oasis.

It is difficult to believe how this huge tree of excellence was started. Seth Shivnarainji Birla started a *pathshala* in Pilani with one teacher for educating his grandsons, late Shri GD Birla and late Shri RD Birla in 1901—that is a hundred and twenty years ago. This small pathshala grew to become a high school and later on an intermediate college. With such a humble beginning, this journey of excellence in education started.

The Birla Education Trust was founded and the intermediate college was converted into a degree college, and later on, postgraduate courses were started.

After Independence, for the next five years, a campus took shape and courses in arts and commerce, as well as pharmacy, were started between 1947 and1952.

It became an institute in 1964 and was named Birla Institute of Technology and Science (BITS).

In the desert, the only god is a well.

—Vera Nazarian

The next value addition was done by affiliating with the Massachusetts Institute of Technology (MIT), US, to adopt international standards in education and learn from their best practices, too. The focus was on quality and excellence.

BITS churned out top-class engineers and never compromised on faculty. It put in place a robust selection process to get the best possible students. It worked on quality and not quantity and had only two thousand five hundred student intake for several years. Only in 1999, it increased its input to four thousand because of a greater demand for quality engineers in the country. The focus was on creating engineers to meet the requirements of Indian industry with strong industry ties—a very big, intangible value addition to keep academics aligned to industry needs.

It was now to expand its wings, and BITS moved international with a campus in Dubai. They also opened state-of-the-art campuses in Goa and Hyderabad atthe invitation of the respective governments.

Another value addition was having a pristine Sarswati temple on campus—Birla Mandir, made out of classic marble. Go global but think Indian with Indian values in place. BITS is a township built on a 300-plus-acre campus. The institute has fourteen hostels in total. Each hostel is referred to as a "Bhawan," the Sanskrit word for hostel. Thirteen of them—Krishna Bhawan, Vishwakarma Bhawan, Rana Pratap Bhawan, Bhagirath Bhawan, Ashok Bhawan, Gandhi Bhawan, Shankar Bhawan, Vyas Bhawan, Budh Bhawan, Ram Bhawan, Pandit Madan Mohan Malviya Bhawan, CV Raman Bhawan, and Srinivasa Ramanujan Bhawan are for male students. There is a single hostel for female students called Meera Bhawan. All hostels are named after saints, scientists, and historical and religious figures from India.

Value addition is done gradually and by several people in the case of a large organization. Therefore, if you get a chance to lead an organization or even a small department, you must contribute your bit and add your contribution to organizational growth and excellence. Everyone can do value addition in his radius of influence.

BITS has contributed to thenational and international arena, and several alumni have become its torchbearers. Some are listed below.

1. Baba Kalyani, chairman of Bharat Forge and a billionaire.

I am a very hands-on person, and I like to be involved in driving my business.

—Baba Kalyani

2. Sabeer Bhatia, founder of Hotmail.

Don't be afraid to tread new ground, but do a sanity test.

—Sabeer Bhatia

3. SK Roongta, Chairman, SAIL.
4. Goverdhan Mehta, Chairman, NAAC, Government of India.

5. Bala Natarajan, Professor, Kansas State University, USA.

Several other fields like academics (professors at Harvard, Stanford), politics, civil services, and arts also see BITS alumni shining.

It's the adventure, the adrenaline-flowing, risk-taking in outdoor activities that attracts me

—Baba Kalyani

National Institute of Information Technology (NIIT)

We now accept the fact that learning is a lifelong process of keeping abreast of change. And the most pressing task is to teach people how to learn.

—Peter Drucker

Sometimes ideas are started with the idea of value addition to an existing phenomenon or meeting a challenge. Some people sit and watch while others take the initiative and go for it.

Something similar happened when a bunch of IIT graduates (initially only two) realized that information technology had just arrived and people were struggling to handle computers. It was like you had a constant stream of cars, but no one could drive and no one could repair a car or create some of its parts. Cars were there, but someone had to supply the fuel (software) and you needed a driver to drive it (to operate it).

In 1981, when micro computers or desktops and personal computers had hit the market in a big way in India, Rajinder Pawar and Vijay Thadani, both from IIT Delhi, decided to start computer training for beginners. I was that time a student at IIT, Bombay, doing my master's in computer science, where we used to get to work only on mainframe computers. I remember in 1980, IIT Bombay'scomputer science department had bought just four desktop computers. They were delicate, pretty expensive, and kept in an air-conditioned room, and were seemingly (we were told) allergic to dust! To enter that room, one had to book in advance, and it was like entering a *mandir* or a temple.

At that time, the computer was like an enigma for a graduate or a postgraduate and the corporate world too. They looked at it as something that was beyond them and highly technical. But people wanted to learn, and there was nowhere to go. Pawar and Thadani took advantage of this demand and realized the business potential, and with just 100,000 INR they started their venture. Later, many IITians joined this venture, and a senior person from this venture, who himself is from IIT, Delhi, told me that the name NIIT was thought of as a group of IIT guys or N number of IIT guys—NIITians.

NIIT conceived a franchising model in IT education for the very first time, setting up nine centers by 1987. This was the first direct business value addition. The business took off like wildfire. There was a huge demand and no competition forsuch a competent team.

One learns from books and examples only that certain things can be done. Actual learning requires that you do those things.

—Frank Herbert

Within five years, they were sailing(with a lot of effort), and by 1986, NIIT began its foray into the software domain, beginning with software product distribution under the Insoft brand. The company also began offering advice and consultancy to large corporations on how to leverage technology and make optimum use of their IT investments.

From here on, there was a string of value additions to the entire value chain in software, and they saw growth thatcan be divided into three distinct phases. 1981 to 1990 was the initial phase and 1991 to 2000 was the growth phase. By 1995, revenue crossed the Rs. 1 billion mark. From 2000 onward, it was an expansion phase, and they kept adding value to quality and services. In 2001, NIIT launched an experiment that was christened "Hole-in-the-Wall" by the media and drew international attention. The experiment was based on the "minimally invasive education" methodology developed by NIIT's R&D team. It suggested that children, irrespective of their social, ethnic, or educational identity, could learn to use computers by themselves, without adult intervention. This was a perfect way to penetrate rural and semiurban areas. In 2004, NIIT hived off its software business into an independent organization called NIIT Technologies Ltd. In 2009, NIIT University (NU), a not-for-profit university, was established.

Yet another feather in the cap—in 2014, NIIT tied up with National Skill Development Corporation to launch NIIT YuvaJyoti centers under the pilot phase of Prime Minister Narendra Modi's Skill India campaign and the Pradhan Mantri Kaushal Vikas Yojana (PMKVY) in the North East, Jammu and Kashmir, and Jharkhand.

Tell me and I forget, teach me and I may remember, involve me and I learn.

—Benjamin Franklin

Symbiosis The story of a great man who took an initiative to change the Indian education scenario

If You are planning for a year, sow rice; if you are planning for a decade, plant trees; if you are planning for a lifetime, educate people

—Chinese Proverb

I have witnessed it, being a part of the organization for ten long years as the director of a management institute at Symbiosis University, Pune, India. Working with Dr. SB Mujumdar, the chancellor and founder of Symbiosis, was the best of my professional years.

A clear headed person with a long-term vision, a perfect gentleman, and very unassuming, Dr. Mujumdar is definitely first amongst his equals. Today a University with around 50 Institutes/ colleges/schools with a brand equity of sorts, which was started by Dr. Mujumdar as a small initiative of an educationist like him who left a comfortable job to start this venture.

He had joined Fergusson College, Pune, as professor and head of department in botany, a position he held for twenty years. He was a recognized postgraduate teacher and a guide for PhD students.

He was a member of the Pune University's Executive Council, the Senate, Academic Council (for fourteenyears), and chairman of the Board of Studies in Botany (for nineyears). He was also the Indian Council for Cultural Relations' (ICCR)foreign academic advisor at Pune University (for sevenyears). He has published over fifty original research articles in several national and international scientific journals. He has authored several books on life sciences and has contributed over two hundred articles on science, education, and youth development. He has also been the chairman of the Educational Wing of the Federation of Indian Chambers of Commerce & Industry (FICCI) in 2005–2006.

It's not that I'm so smart, it's just that I stay with problems longer.

—Albert Einstein

How it All Started

Deeply touched by the hardships suffered by foreign students—especially Afro-Asian students—studying in Pune in Maharashtra, in 1971, he established Symbiosis with a view to help them and provide them a "home away from home." He soon realized that education is the best medium for promoting international understanding. This initiative was then pushed forward with value addition.

He started establishing educational institutions imparting quality instruction in diverse disciplines, e. g., English language teaching, management, law, IT, computers, engineering, international business, geo-informatics, media & communication, and photography, etc.

Symbiosis started very small, with probably a small presence on Senapati Bapat Road, and being a teacher, Mujumdar didn't have much money to invest. But the blueprint in his mind was much bigger. He started moving one step at a time and concentrated only on quality education and nothing else. The pace of value addition is very important. If a cake takes two hours to bake, you cannot bake it in thirty minutes by increasing the temperature of the oven by four times—you will burn it! This is the first important lesson—that you need to bite off as much as you can chew.

Another important thing is that he was never after making more money. It came automatically as the product was good. The product of an educational institute is the students. Therefore, the guiding principle that evolved with his initiative was to take the best students based on a fair selection process and then work on them to make them shining stars. That was the success mantra. Most educational institutes in India fail because they indiscriminately admit students and then don't spend efforts on making them better. Even if you do, you cannot make a stallion out of an unhealthy horse. Garbage in is garbage out. People don't understand this simple logic. Software, i.e., the faculty and curriculum, is more important than, hardware, i.e., swanky buildings and campus. That should follow; don't put the cart in front of the horse. Symbiosis doesn't advertise on TV or even in the print media, except for the mandatory notices for admissions. Others who spend millions on TV spots are still lagging behind. Honesty, dedication, and giving value for money to students, along with a robust, unbiased selection process, are what made a small initiative into an education conglomerate.

An investment in knowledge pays the best interest.

—Benjamin Franklin

Symbiosis has around thirty-two thousand students from across India and eighty-five foreign counties. The Ministry of HRD, Government of India, conferred upon Symbiosis in 2002 the status of "Deemed to be University." Many Symbiosis institutions are ranked amongst the top ten institutions in India and they have a placement record of almost 100 percent. What is the point of an education that does not make you job-ready? Realizing the importance of distance education, Symbiosis has established Symbiosis Centre for Distance Learning (SCDL), which conducts a number of online courses and has over two hundred thousand students from India as well as many foreign countries. It has recently focused on skill development and has started a skill development university too.

All Symbiosis institutions are generally need-based. These are run on and adhere to the best ethical practices. The faculty is selected purely on merit and without considerations of caste, creed, religion, or region. One of the unique institutions established by Symbiosis is Symbiosis Institute of Management Studies (SIMS) which provides management education exclusively for children of defense personnel. Another innovative institution is the Pune Police Public School, managed by Symbiosis, which provides education to the children of police personnel. Apart from these academic activities, Symbiosis has also established a magnificent Dr. Ambedkar Museum and Memorial, which houses the personal belongings and memorabilia of Dr. Baba Saheb Ambedkar. It has also established an Afro-Asian Cultural Museum.

College was especially sweet because of the positive, hopeful atmosphere of a college campus.

—Jerry Kramer

Indian Institute of Science (IISc) A hundred-year-old legacy

Common people have an appetite for food, uncommon people have an appetite for service.

—JRD Tata

It was during a chance meeting between Swami Vivekananda and Jamsetji Tata on a ship as co-passengers on a ship journey from Japan to Chicago in 1893 when intellectual patriotic talk started between two great people of India. Tata wanted to bring the steel Industry to India in a big way.

Impressed by the intellect and enthusiasm of Vivekananda during the discussion, about five years later, Mr. Tata wrote a letter to Swami Vivekananda about his idea of starting a science research institute in India and wanted him to help him establish that.

Vivekananda endorsed the project with enthusiasm, and Tata, with the aim of advancing the scientific capabilities of the country, constituted a Provisional Committee to prepare a plan for setting up an institute of research and higher education. A draft proposal was put up to Lord Curzon in December 1898. Subsequently, Sir William Ramsay, a Nobel Laureate, was called on to propose a suitable place for such an institution; he suggested Bangalore as the best location. Bangalore metall the broad parameters for an institute of high value. It had a great climate and greenery. It was an initiative taken by one man, Jamsetji Tata, and supported by several like-minded people.

When you work, work as if everything depends on you. When you pray; pray as if everything depends on God.

—JRD Tata

The land and other facilities for the institution were donated on behalf of the state of Mysore and Tata himself. The state of Karnataka donated a land parcel of around 370 acres and also contributed Rs. 5,00,000 (now valued atRs. 12.5 million) toward capital expenditure and Rs. 50,000 (now valued at Rs. 1.25 million) for annual expenses. The foundation was laid in early 1911, and the first batch was admitted by the end of July of the same year. Now that the institute had started in all earnestness, a lot of great minds collaborated to keep adding value—in this case, intellectual value of high quality—to do research in pure sciences and technology. The initial years were supported by foreign scientists as departmental heads and the director of the institute. The first Indian director was the Nobel Laureate Sir C. V. Raman. The institute was the first to introduce master's programs in engineering. Very soon, it also started integrated doctoral programs in physical, biological, chemical, and mathematical sciences. It became the topmost research institute in pure science.

In 1958, the institute was granted deemed university status by the University Grants Commission (UGC).

It is a lush, green, fully residential institute with a state-of-theart library and computing facilities. A number of other research institutes—Raman Research Institute, Indian Space Research

Organization (ISRO), Wood Research Institute, and Central Power Research Institute (CPRI)—are close to IISc, which was like a mother institute for research in India. As a result of this, Defence Research and Development Organisation (DRDO) labs have also come up in Bangalore, in a township called CV Raman Nagar. Once a critical mass is achieved, others get pulled into it. No wonder Bangalore has become the Silicon Valley of India. Several other top colleges, including the Indian Institute of Management, Bangalore (IIMB), a top management Institute in India, the Indian Statistical Institute (ISI), the Indian Institute of Astrophysics, National Institute of Advance Studies (NIAS), the National Law School (NLSIU), the Indian Institute of Theoretical Sciences, National Institute of Design (NID), and National Institute of Fashion Technology (NIFT), have come up in the city. In addition, biotechnology is a rapidly expanding field in the city.

Before Bangalore was called the Silicon Valley of India, the city made its name as headquarters to some of the largest public sector heavy industries of India. The Hindustan Aeronautics Limited (HAL) headquarters is in Bangalore and is dedicated to research and development activities for indigenous fighter aircraft for the Indian Air Force. With over nine thousand five hundred employees, it is one of the largest public sector employers in Bangalore.

Other heavy industries in Bangalore include Bharat Electronics Limited, Bharat Heavy Electricals Limited (BHEL), Indian Telephone Industries (ITI), Bharat Earth Movers Limited (BEML), HMT (formerly Hindustan Machine Tools), Hindustan Motors (HM), Manjushree Technopack, and the ABB Group.

The economy of Bangalore contributes over 87 percent to the economy of the state of Karnataka, the majority of it coming from the software industry.

Several people, including JRD Tata and the government, did a value addition, and that is how it has become a city of excellence, starting from IISc. Bangalore was not built in a day.

People did value addition to IISc, and IISC did value addition to Bangalore.

In a day, when you don't come across any problems— you can be sure that you are travelling on a wrong path.

—Swami Vivekananda

The Stanford Story

An idea triggered in their heart becomes a mammoth initiative

Nomatter how good you get, you can always get better and that's the exciting part.

—Tiger Woods, alumnus of Stanford

Rome was not built in a day—but someone started the process. According to tradition, on April 21, 753 BC, Romulus and his twin brother, Remus, found Rome on the site where they were suckled by a she-wolf as orphaned infants. If this myth is to be believed, the foundation of modern-day Rome was laid 2,750 years ago. As new rulers came, they all did some value addition, and that is why Rome is what it is today. Like great cities, great institutes take time to build.

Stanford University, one of the world's most reputed institutions of education, also had a humble beginning. It was benevolent leadership in education. The Leland Stanford Junior University was founded in 1885 by Jane and Leland Stanford in memory of their only child, Leland Jr., who died of typhoid fever at the age of fifteen. After his death, the Stanfords determined that they would use their wealth to do something for other people's children. In fact, within a few hours of his son's death, Stanford said to his wife, "The children of California shall be our children." That was the beginning of Stanford University.

Leland Stanford was the former governor of California and was a very rich man, a business tycoon in the railroad business. He bought the first of what would become more than 8,000 acres of land as big as the National Defense Academy (NDA) in India, on the San Francisco peninsula where Harvard was founded.

The idea was to create a university with a different DNA—something untraditional. It would be coeducational at a time when most private universities were all-male. Most were associated with a religious organization. They wanted it to be different and aimed at producing cultured and useful citizens.

The vision was, "To qualify its students for personal success, and direct usefulness in life" and its purpose, "To promote the public welfare by exercising an influence on behalf of humanity and civilization."

They specified in the founding grant that the buildings should "be like the old adobe houses of the early Spanish days; they will be one-storied; they will have deep window seats and open fireplaces, and the roofs will be covered with the familiar dark red tiles." This is called getting passionately involved in a project and giving it a different look and feel. Renowned landscape architect Frederick Law Olmsted designed the campus.

After the demise of Leland Stanford in 1893, Stanford University struggled financially. After World War II, Provost Frederick Terman supported faculty and graduates' entrepreneurialism to build a selfsufficient local industry in what would later be known as Silicon Valley. Institutions and ideas are great if they can cause a ripple effect. Stanford University did that in a big way, contributing to the personal growth of students by augmenting their Prosperity Quotient and also creating a massive industry base to add to the GDP of America. Some of the noted alumni are:

Sergey Brin. *Hewas a PhD candidate at Stanford University before he and* **Larry Page** *founded Google in 1998.*

Always deliver more than expected.

—Larry Page

Mukesh Ambani. He is India's richest person and the chairman, managing director, and largest shareholder of Reliance Industries Limited (RIL). After graduating from the University of Bombay with a degree in chemical engineering, he attended Stanford University's business school before leaving in 1981 to work at RIL.

The organizational architecture is really that a centipede walks on hundred legs and one or two don't count. So, if I lose one or two legs, the process will go on, the organization will go on, the growth will go on.

—Mukesh Ambani, Chairman, Reliance Industry

Yahoo CEO,**Marissa Mayer,** who loved computer science and computer programming, graduated with a BS in 1997 and an MS in 1999.

Instagram co-founder and CEO, **Kevin Systrom,** graduated from Stanford in 2006 with a degree in management science and engineering, and had his first foray into the professional world as an intern at the start-up, Odeo, which would later become Twitter.

Stanford's contribution to sports too is note worthy. **Tiger Woods'** golf career was already off to an impressive start while he was a student at Stanford University, where he won numerous awards. Woods studied economics for two years and left the university in 1995 to play golf professionally.

I love to compete. That's the essence of who I am.

—Tiger Woods

As of April 2021, the university has created eighty-four Nobel laureates, twenty-nine Turing Award laureates who are alumni, faculty, or staff. Stanford is also famous for its entrepreneurship programs and incubation and is one of the most successful universities in attracting funding for start-ups.

Stanford alumni have founded numerous companies, which combined produce more than $2.7 trillion in annual revenue and have created more than six million jobs, roughly equivalent to the seventh largest economy in the world. Stanford University has 5,580 alumni who are millionaires, with a total wealth of $2,899 billion.

The university is the alma mater of one president of the United States (Herbert Hoover), seventy-four living billionaires, and seventeen astronauts. It is also one of the leading producers of Fulbright Scholars, Marshall Scholars, and Rhodes Scholars.

Economic depression cannot be cured by legislative action or executive pronouncement. Economic wounds must be healed by the action of the cells of the economic body - the producers and consumers themselves.

—Herbert Hoover, Former US President

6
Great Companies

HE REARE FOUR stories of people who created business with initiative, value addition, and innovation.

Amul
"The Taste of India"

Amul is one of the best examples of initiatives by one man and then great value addition by another. Today, this brand needs no introduction and has achieved this with great vision backed bysolid leadership and the hard work of every individual. It was the pride of the people and today the pride of the nation. The top management is constantly innovating and doing value addition to its product line. As they say, "Change is the only constant." The revenue growth target for 2019– 20 was20.7 percent to Rs. 40,000 crore and wasexpected to be Rs. 50,000 croresin 2020–21.

How Did it Start?

Amul started with a philanthropic idea—of helping poor farmers who did not get dues for the milk they produced and found it hard to market it. Most often, the middlemen wiped out the money, which rightfully belonged to farmers.

In 1946, Tribhuvandas Kishibhai Patel started a revolution to help poor dairy farmers and landless laborers. He gathered several farmers from neighboring areas and villages in Anand, a township in the state of Gujarat, and met Vallabhbhai Patel (former deputy prime minister of India), who suggested that they form a cooperative of their own. During that time, Polson was the only brand for dairy products in India and was exploiting Indian dairy farmers.

Obviously, Polson tried to resist, but the cooperative with all the farmers backing it succeeded, and Polson had to give in. Thus, the initiative of one man gave birth to an organization.

Dr. Verghese Kurien stepped into the scene as manager and guided them to form a very successful cooperative, and this was a great value addition. This small cooperative grew to become a huge, popular Indian brand, which is very well-received both in India and abroad. Amul helped India to become the world's largest producer of milk. This was also called the White Revolution. Remember, any revolution or evolution starts with the first step, which is the initiative. Any farmer was free to join the cooperative union irrespective of his or her caste, religion, or financial status. Today, Amul has a total of thirty-oneplants in India.

The name Amul is an acronym for Anand Milk Union Limited, which was given by Dr. Kurian atthe suggestion of one of his friends.

Technology plays a pivotal role in the success of Amul, which uses automatic milk collection systems to collect milk from farmers at a swift pace, simultaneously capture details about the farmers and milk, like the lipid content of milk, on a daily basis, and collects around 3.3 million liters of milk from *farmers in villages all across India*. The farmers get paid instantaneously, within a matter of a few seconds.

In fact, there is no single owner of Amul, which is a cooperative society and is jointly owned by 3.6 million milk producers in Gujarat.

Amul has undoubtedly improved the quality of farmers' lives in rural areas in general and the lives of women farmers in particular.

Kanuben Patel of Gujarat was awarded the Pride of Gujarat by the chief minister of Gujarat for proving that dairy farming is a very viable business. She made around Rs. 84 lakhs or 8.4 million INR by dairy farming.

The milk is examined for purity and contamination, then scientifically graded and transported to many dairies located across the country. The milk delivery trucks deliver milk during the early morning to every nook and corner of the country. These activities occur daily with clock work precision with the use of technology.

The main pillars in the success of Amul are the conjunction of expertise of farmers and the professionalism of the cooperative's management and technology.

This made India the largest milk-producing nation in the world and brought financial freedom to farmers. Another reason for the huge success of Amul is their diversification into numerous dairy based products like ice-creams, chocolates, etc. All Amul's products adhere to the strict hygiene and quality standards. *Amul products are not only the bestin class but also very affordable.*

Amul'sis a very clean and fair system—fair to the farmers and also to the buyers. It is a win-win situation for everyone.

One must appreciate that by being fair to all, you can still make great profits.

Value Addition in Agribusiness is Very Profitable

Youth need to take the initiative and do value addition to their produce

There is a constant clamor that Indian farmers are very poor and that governments are wasting crores every year to give them incentives, easy loans, and even loan waivers, yet there is still no solution in sight. However, some youth in our country used their education, ability to learn,and initiative and delivered value-added products to createa profitable business.

Devesh Patel, an IT graduate in Anand, Gujarat, is an interesting case study of how agriculture can become a very profitable business. Here is his story in brief.

His father and grandfather were farmers and own 12 acres of land in their village, which is by no means a big land parcel. It comes to approximately five hectares. What good is your education if you can't take your family business to new heights? Education should give you the ability to value add to any line of work you undertake—and it does give you that ability—but it depends on an individual alone as to what and how much he does with his education.

Patel did not take up a job. Instead, he decided to work on his farm and take it to a different level, and he did it. He took the initiative to do something different, whereas most of his classmates tookup jobs in cities.

He is a great believer in making theproduct better and better by doing value additions to theproduce.

He says that in one hectare of land, in eightto ninemonths, he gets 300 to 400 quintals (one quintal is 100 kg) of *haldi* (turmeric). If he sells it raw in the market, he gets only fourto sixlakh rupeesfor the entire crop, and there is also a problem in the *mandi* or market, where you are at the mercy of the middlemen. His expense for one hectare is Rs. 1.75 lakhs.

Actually, this is the biggest problem for farmers, and that is why, despite all government efforts, farmers who toil hard end up as paupers and are poor throughout their lives. This is a big deterrent for anyone to go into farming. It is never seen as a good business. This perception of *garibkisan* or poor farmer whom everyone pities should go.

How to mitigate this risk and hedge his losses and boost profits was Patel'sbiggest challenge. His mantra is value addition. I remember in one of his speeches, PM Narendra Modi also said, "We must do value addition. You can make mango pickle and sell it better than raw mango; if you bottle it, you get more money, and if you put a nice picture of a model and a good brand name, which looks neatly packed, you get a multiplication factor of three or thereabout."

This is basic common sense; unfortunately, in India, we never pay attention to this. Patel got the right pulse of the customer and marketing dynamics and he went hammer and tongs to formulate his strategy. How else could he capture foreign markets? Today, 40 percent of his produce is exported!

He uses traditional manure, using cow dung and urine, to grow organic produce, and has created a standard procedure to make this.

He washes the raw turmeric, steams it at 100 degrees Celsius, follows a twenty-two-day drying process, removes skin and any dirt, polishes it through a machine, and then packs it in 500 gm to 50 kg packets, labels them, and sells. The turmeric can also be pulverized and made into powder. This value addition costs him about Rs. 75,000 extra, but he sells it for 18 to 20 lakh rupees.

A similar process is done for producing high-quality ginger. Ginger gets him Rs. 32 lakhs per hectare. He says one can make ginger powder, ginger paste, or ginger *masala* tea. Once packed, there is no hurry to sell because packed goods have a much longer shelf life than raw ginger or turmeric.

He has created his own automatic polishing machine, which has bamboo baskets and does the polishing in the most natural way. These are electromechanically operated, mounted on a tabletop type of steel structure. He has designed it and shared that design with a local workshop that now makes it in different sizes and capacities for other farmers too. This is what happens when you progress. You help yourself and create livelihoods for others too.

Patelis very quality conscious. He looks after the production, and his wife looks after the packaging, labeling, and marketing. He has used his IT knowledge and created a wonderful website. He has a Facebook page which has helped him reach out to bigger markets and showcase his products to sell in foreign markets too. He has mastered the art of marketing and sells directly to customers through an online platform. They have five cows and animals on the farm. They get milk as well as fertilizers.

The Wipro Story: A Journey of Consistent Value Addition

Azim Premji—from rich to superrich

Use your mind to think about things, rather than think of them. You want to be adding value as you think about projects and people, not simply reminding yourself they exist.

—David Allen

What is the point if a young man born in a rich family goes and studies in one of the best colleges and does not grow that company? There are many stories of rags to riches and many more who turned riches into ashes—born to rich parents but drained the entire wealth in wine, woman, and fun. They not only disgraced the family but got themselves into trouble, often landing up as alcoholic, debauched paupers.

AzimPremji did exactly the opposite. He had gone to do his engineering from the prestigious Stanford University in the United States. His father had established Wipro as Western Indian Vegetable Products Ltd. in 1945 at Bombay—now Mumbai-. It was a business worth a couple of million dollars and was mainly producing hydrogenated edible oil. The company was also into the rice business.

His father, unfortunately, expired before he could finish his education, and he returned to Mumbai at the tender age of twenty-one. He obviously inherited the company and his father's fortune and took the reins of the business. He was ticked off by a company shareholder in a shareholders' meeting, complaining that at twenty-onehe was too young to handle such a complex business. Premji decided that day to work harder, and spent most of his time in the factory and office to understand things better.

Not only did he handle the existing business well, but he also did a lot of value addition to the existing business. When IBM, the American computer giant, left India on the behest of the then government in 1980, Premji thought of using this as a business opportunity.

He quickly got into manufacturing personal computers (PC). PCs had just become known in the market, but it was definitely a lucrative market. The company started with manufacturing microcomputers under a technology-sharing agreement with US-based Sentinel Computers. Later, it started providing software solutions to complement its hardware operations. Premjihired the best people for his company and understood that good, qualified, hardworking, technical manpower was available in India thatwas much cheaper than American manpower. He used this to his advantage, and as IT stocks went up, his fortune multiplied. He kept adding other related business lines to his core IT business (value addition). He also opened a business process outsourcing (BPO) unit in 2002 and the company was one of the best-performing stocks during 1998–2003 on the Indian stock exchanges. Premji created a culture of striving for excellence in business operations, and Wipro was successful in implementing the objectives that were part of this culture, being one of the first software companies to get SEI Level 5 certification.

If you invest and don't diversify, you're literally throwing out money. People don't realize that diversification is beneficial even if it reduces your return. Why? Because it reduces your risk even more. Therefore, if you diversify and then use margin to increase your leverage to a risk level equivalent to that of a non-diversified position, your return will probably be greater.

—Jeff Yass

He diversified into providing software solutions and other services to American clients and other big customers abroad. He invested in training his people to get the best results and a competitive edge over other players in the market. In 1999, Premji officially completed his degree from Stanford through a distance-learning arrangement— another value addition to his persona.

Following India's economic deregulation in 1991, Wipro further diversified into the manufacturing of lamps, powders, oil-based natural ingredients, medical and diagnostic equipment, and IT hardware products such as printers and scanners. It also entered the IT services business in the 1990s and was among the first to experiment with offshore IT services. In 1999, Wipro became the only Indian computer manufacturer to receive Y2K-compliant certification from the National Software Testing Laboratory in the US. It also entered into a joint venture with KPN Telecom

(Netherlands) to provide internet services in India (another diversification). The following year saw Wipro list in the US via American Depositary Receipts and emerge as one of India's largest software exporters and the second-largest listed company in India. One major lesson here is: Always stick to your core competence and grow business lines around it, ensuring that the dots always remain connected; don't start totally alien business models.

AzimPremji is one of India's most well-known and respected business leaders and has received many awards during his lifetime, most notably India's second-highest civilian honor for his contribution to business. He was also selected as one of the 30 Greatest Global Entrepreneurs of all time by *Business Week* and was named one of the 100 most influential people in the world.

All wealth comes from adding value, from producing more, better, cheaper, faster, and easier than someone else.

—Brian Tracy

Premji transformed Wipro under his leadership from a $2 million cooking fat company into a conglomerate spanning multiple businesses that consistently generate billions of dollars in revenue each year. Premji is indeed one of the pioneers in developing the IT sector in India and putting the sector on the global stage. Something else that is noteworthy about Azim Premji is that he has managed to build an organization that has a reputation for being an ethical company committed to certain core values, and he has taken a keen interest in creating high-performance teams.

Mr. Premjiis known for his effective management and business skills. He believes that to achieve success in life you must have hardwork, perseverance, and honesty. We usually don't give attention to these things in life.

A Large-Hearted Man

One of the many reasons that Premji will be remembered is for his contribution to charity. He has already given away $21 billion of his wealth as part of the Giving Pledge, a commitment by the world's wealthiest individuals to donate the majority of their wealth to charitable causes. Premji was the first Indian and only the third non- American to make this pledge.

This includes two-thirds of his Wipro stock, which has been placed in a separate trust and will be used for educational purposes. The AzimPremji Foundation was set up as a nonprofit organization in 2001 with the aim of improving primary education in India. It has also set up a university in Bengaluru, India, and works with schools and governments in various districts of India to improve education in a holistic way, rather than just through financing.

Azim Premji is a role model of diversification and value addition to an existing business, who turned a small, family-owned cookingoil company into Wipro Limited, a multinational conglomerate focused on providing technology outsourcing services.

I strongly believe that those of us, who are privileged to have wealth, should contribute significantly to try and create a better world for the millions who are far less privileged.

—AzimPremji

Honda

If you make a superior product, people will buy it.

—Soichiro Honda

Brands are created with initiative and nurtured and sustained with constant value addition. The journey of Soichiro Honda—a rags-toriches story—is worth reading in this context.

All of us would have owned a Honda two-wheeler or a car or at least taken ridden in one sometime or the other. I have yet to meet a person who owned a Honda vehicle and ever complained about it. Everyone loves a Honda vehicle—from a scooter to a zipping bike to a luxury car. It is a dominant and one of the most reliable names in the automobile industry today.

At fifteen, without any formal education, Soichiro left home and headed to Tokyo to look for work. He obtained an apprenticeship at a garage in 1922. After some hesitation over his employment, he stayed for six years, working as a car mechanic before returning home to start his own auto repair business in 1928.

Honda was neither good nor was he interested in studies. He worked with his father in his cycle repair shop. He was an inquisitive boy, and from childhood, was keen to learn how engines worked and machines were made. He started small by making piston rings for Toyota, which was his dream company. To learn the ropes, he interned with smaller garages and joined an engineering college to seek knowledge and not a paper degree. He attended only practical classes and left engineering studies halfway.

Honda had developed a revolutionary engine piston ring, and all he wanted to do was work in the assembly line at Toyota. That was his dream. He worked day and night in his small workshop to make this dream a reality—even selling his wife's jewelry and sleeping many nights alone in his workshop. Once Honda had made his piston ring, he took it to Toyota. However, he was rejected because they said it didn't meet their high standards of engineering. He was ready to make improvements to his product.

I would have to put in the necessary time, but nothing could stop me from succeeding.

—Soichiro Honda

Undeterred, Honda enrolled in a technical school with a single goal— to figure out why he couldn't produce apiston ring of the required quality. After two years of redesigning, he finally came up with a piston ring that was of the quality Toyota had asked for. He was given a contract, but he needed a factory to manufacture the piston rings. The piston rings could be used for cars, motorbikes, and airplanes, but this was not an ideal time at all—the Japanese government was gearing up for war against the United States. Honda simply couldn't source the materials needed to build his factory. He did manage to build a small manufacturing plant for this, which got destroyed twice over—once due to war bombing and the second time due to an earthquake.

After World War II, Honda realized that petrol was expensive and not easily available. Therefore, he decided to make transportation cheaper and more fuel efficient. He took an old petrol engine and mounted it on his cycle. It worked well and was very efficient. He began to test his new "motorized bicycle" around the town, and friends quickly asked if they could haveone too. He was flooded with requests for his new invention. It seemed as if Honda was back in business.

However, with Japan's economy in shambles after the war, it was difficult to get investors. Honda needed investment to produce the new "scooters." He wrote to a large number of cycle shop owners to join his effort, and three thousand bicycle shop owners responded. He formed strategic alliances with them and helped them see how he could increase their bike sales. Suffice it to say he got more than enough of the money he needed to build his new scooters.

I will become the Napoleon of mechanics!

—Soichiro Honda

From these extremely challenging circumstances, Honda has now become one of the most pioneering companies in the world and is still the world's largest motorcycle maker. It employs over two hundred thousand people worldwide and has revenues of over $10 billion a year. But it was all made possible through one man's initiative and his determination in the face of almost unimaginable odds.

After the war, Honda became reacquainted with his friend Takeo Fujisawa, whom he had known during his days as a supplier of piston rings to Nakajima Aircraft Company. In 1949, Honda hired Fujisawa, who oversaw the financial side of the company and helped the firm expand. In 1959, Honda Motorcycles opened its first dealership in the United States.

As president of the Honda Motor Company, Soichiro Honda turned the company into a billion-dollar multinational that produced the best-selling motorcycles in the world. Honda's engineering and marketing skills resulted in Honda motorcycles outselling Triumph and Harley-Davidson in their respective home markets.

He took the initiative by going for piston rings, then small contraption bikes, then did value addition to each product and also to his product lines.

I let no one disturb my concentration . . . Even hunger could not disturb me.

—Soichiro Honda

7

What Your Zodiac Sign Says for you

Your Basic Character

ARIES

Superman and superwoman, who can propel themselves in any direction, are good metaphors of Aries energy. Fire is a process that causes change, and Aries use energy to bring about changes. Aries is the most energetic ofthe fire signs and usually takes the initiative by always being in the front.

I can be likened to a fire that gives direction, such as in a rocket, a gun, or an engine. I am a person of action, and this may sometimes make me act first and think later about what I really should have done instead. My ability to be active and dynamic are wonderful qualities, but my impulsive and outgoing energy can sometimes act without reflection. I am able to take decisions—fast decisions—without looking up to the authority of my superiors.

Take care:

- You are ready to take initiatives as you have the mindset to comefirst everywhere. This is a great quality.
- You take initiatives and expect others to follow it—you bring about change in people as well as organizations and always do value addition wherever you go.
- You are at times impulsive and aggressive in nature, which can sometimes affect your relationships with friends and can also affectyour work.
- You sometimes lack caution, being by nature an impulsive person, and you are too quick in thought and action.

Taurus

Taureans generally grasp new ideas slowly as they are agains tchange. Innovation will not cross their minds or occupy them unles sit is well established that it could lead to better results. Once innovative ideas are espoused and comprehended, Taureans come out as strongsupporters and could also lead the movement. They might consider it as a foundation and stick to it all their life. They aren't interested intaking unwanted risks that can put their solid footing in jeopardy. Taureans are one of the most practical signs, but they do take time toadjust to the learning curve. The reason being that they are very fixedin their opinions and hence fail to see the virtues of other people'sarguments.

As I generally follow reliable patterns of experience and am more practical than intellectual, value addition happens in a very limited scope. I tend to have an air of being stubborn, which generallygives the feeling that I am not open to ideas. But in actuality, I am allears to the suggestion with all its pros and cons before considering it asa value addition to my plan.

Take care:

- You are a little slow to accept or change new ideas and things. This makes you less innovative.

- You need to develop that intellectual side of yours in case you want to do actual value addition.
- You must be a little flexible about your opinions because you willnot be able to bring new things to your organization or yourself.

Gemini

I grasp new ideas readily. I am highly open to innovations and love changes in life and in relationships. I take the initiative to start a new venture, but many times, I am unable to put in sustained effort to complete the project. Either I get tired or bored of my monotonous work or give up at the end because of my restlessness. I am like a youthful kid and have a child in me who is always ready to run anerrand or two at the same time. My mind can bounce around from one topic to another with great ease. I like to keep on rolling and trying new things and am full of initiatives in all the different things that Ideal with.

Take care:

- You are a restless soul and can get disillusioned halfway through the initiative that you have taken.
- You are quite hardworking, but you lack patience and consistency.
- People may find you to be fickle-minded and not very dependable at times because of this. Be careful.

Cancer

I am a cardinal sign. I lead and do not follow. I take the initiatives when there is no one to do so and provide the necessary path for othersto follow. I can be an excellent organizer with a good sense of value and economy, which I may combine with a flair for inventiveness and originality. I can add value to the tasks that I perform by deriving from past experiences or learning from others' mistakes.

Take care:

- You are sometimes over imaginative and even prone to fantasy. You may become unrealistic while defining your goals and aspirations.
- Take care of this.

Leo

I was born to lead and am most effective in a position of command.

I love to take the initiative in any front, be it academics, extra curricular activities, or work. I can organize, hand out duties, and give directionto a group. I have the most remarkable power in building and even manipulating public opinion and in swaying great audiences. People around me look up to me to lead the way in difficult situations. Being a leader of the pack, I am strict about rules, and do not like anyone not taking their work seriously. I am ambitious by nature and prefer to take charge and also delegate.

Take care:

- Guard against snobbish superiority and an over bearing attitude.
- Be patient with others, especially while working in a group.
- You tend to dominate others. This needs to be checked.
- You are pretty clear headed in your approach toward life.

Virgo

The Virgo's careful approach to finances will help build them a sizeable fortune. This, they will invest wisely, usually in areas where there is little risk. If they are encouraged to speculate, they might back a small business or put their money into low-risk investments.

We are better subordinates than leaders. Responsibility irks me, and I often lack the breadth of strategic vision that a leader needs. But I am a truth seeker who loves to discuss ideas. I am a perfectionist who is also cautious and serious. I am methodical, analytical, and critical. I have perseverance. I have good organizational skills. I am kind, concerned, and responsible, and therefore, I will contribute my bit wherever desirable. I have the patience and astuteness to know how to make my money work for me. I also do well in partnership ventures.

I am a hard worker. It is unlikely that money will come to me through anything but hard and purposeful efforts. Deep down, I probably wouldn't want it any other way. One other thing that can be said of me is that I fully appreciate the value of my savings. By the same token, if Iwere to come into a large sum—an inheritance, bonus, lottery win, or awindfall—this isn't likely to go to my head. Instead, I would be careful to invest it wisely for the benefit of my family and close friends.

Take care:

- You need to develop a habit to lead by taking initiative wherever and whenever possible.
- Look at the bigger picture and contribute on a larger scale rather than at a tactical level.

Libra

I can take good initiatives, which come naturally to me as I am full of ideas.

The problem is that I am not too consistent, so I need someone else to carry on with the work that I have started on my own. I am usually a kick-start and not a self-start. I am a social being, and I like to work for society. I am artistic by nature, so I am a creative thinker. It helps me to think out of the box and I can generate ideas for any purpose and condition. I can be a good planner and can do immense value addition to an organization in terms of strategy planning.

Take care:

- You should realize that being a strategy planner is a great strength and you can utilize it not only for professional work but for other purposes too.
- You can develop your artistic side if you give it a serious

thought.

- You can use this trait to get instant recognition and the attention of others.
- You are very lazy and require constant pushing to move forward.

Scorpio

Their deep, incisive, and analytical mind makes them natural detectives.

Also, Scorpios are frequently workaholics—cramming each work day with hours of productiveness.

I am an excellent, relentless worker and excel in anything that I indulge in. I don't take unwanted risks that canput my solid footing in jeopardy. When in a team, I am the most dependable one and provide a lot of value addition by working hard toward the set goal. I learn from my past mistakes and try to improve myself constantly. I generally take a scientific approach to my work.

I take the initiative when I am absolutely sure that it is time. As I am a deep thinker, I think at least a hundred times before getting to the forefront. This slows me down at times, even pushing me behind others, and suppresses my innovativeness.

Take care:

- You may spend a lot of time planning and waiting for the right moment before you act. This may delay your projects and affect your progress negatively. Try to be agile in taking decisions.
- You try to control every situation. This may prove negative in the long run, especially while working in a team.

Sagittarius

Sagittarians are natural teachers and philosophers with a talent for expounding the moral principles and laws that seem to explain the universe. This gift enables them to be successful church menon the one hand and scientists on the other. Law and politics also suit them as do public service, social administration, public relations, and advertising. Travel and exploration naturally appealto such restless souls, and if their opportunities are limited, they may find something worthy of travel—and consider a change of scene in the armed forces or through working as a traveling salesman, if needed.

As a Sagittarian, I am adventurous and I would definitely try to gointo a field that suits my interest areas but would not like to take enough initiatives if the work is not according to my desire, and therefore, can hardly add any value to it. Risk-taking and challenges excite me—and under such conditions, I perform the best. I can take the initiative and addvalue to the job at hand if it interests me.

Take care:

- Every job may not offer risk, challenges, and adventure.
- You should learn to put in your best even if the job is mundane and not very exciting. This is a practical way of looking at life.
- Since you are adventurous by nature, you plunge into new ventures without worrying too much about the situation/ venture you are getting into. This is a plus for you.

Capricorn

I am a bit reserved and guarded, and I don't like taking the initiative unlessit is required. I normally wait for things to happen and sometimes need a trigger to get going. Taking the initiative is perceived to be good quality at a workplace, whereby a person can stand out in a crowd, but I normally try to keep a low profile and a guarded approach. As faras the work in hand is concerned, I can perform it better than any one else. So, I must try and take more initiative and try to stand out at my workplace.

Take care:

- You always observe others and their plans and only then make yourplans to beat them.
- You lack initiative, but you always add value to the job that

has been entrusted to you.

- You are a quiet worker and don't like to hog too much limelight.
- Sometimes, you should make efforts to take credit for your hardwork.

Aquarius

As an Aquarian, I am constructive, dedicated, and energetic. This dynamic nature of mine helps me to be decisive and a risk-taker. I am courageous, responsible, motivated, sincere, and confident. All these qualities help me become a trendsetter, innovator, and path finder.

There is always a high craving for knowledge, which makes me a good learner. I am creative, charismatic, and farsighted, and have analyticalability. Thus, this quality of mine is a positive one. So I should keep it as my unique selling point and try and be my original self as faras this trait is concerned. I have a great intellectual gift and an intense desire to communicate with others. I am innovative and inventive, and I often think out of the box. I can be counted upon for generating new ideas and do real value addition to any project that I take up. I am good at electronics, computers, and even social work. As a team mate, I always add value to any group activity. I can help a project or a mission on a long-term basis.

Take care:

- Sometimes, you dream a lot and plan things sitting in an ivory tower. Try to be practical and not theoretical all the time.
- Unless your ego is boosted, you don't give your best. Try to workwithout looking for compliments and being an exhibitionist.
- Sometimes, you are stubborn and rude to your teammates. It may hinder your growth because others may not cooperate for your success. Avoid this.
- You are farsighted, lively, and prepared to do things differently. Keep this up, and always put your best foot forward.

Pisces

A pair of fish represents Pisceans, a symbol that prompts others to suggest that these people "go with the flow" and "don't make waves." Both of these labels are true, since Pisceans are fluid and easy going, in keeping with the mutable quality assigned to this sign. A typical Piscean generally does not take any initiative. He will take initiative only if there is something related to the field of arts or something he has mastery over. A Piscean does not believe in a lot of value addition to enhance his skills and abilities.

I will take the initiative only if it's related to fine arts, writing, or anyother form of art. Generally, I resist taking any initiative. I tend to follow what others do most of the time. I believe that my instinct will lead me and that I need not take the lead myself. I need to take more initiative and take the lead to showcase the various abilities that I possess. I should be prepared for more value addition and learn to assimilate a lot of new things and continue to increase my knowledge base so that I don't get left behind. I must make a conscious effort to learn to initiate not only the things that I am comfortable with but also add value to myself and become a more rounded personality.

Take care:

- A laid-back attitude is your biggest weakness. You can also take it asa positive because you don't suffer those "pangs of ambition."
- You never try to lead but are happy to follow the crowd or the flow.

Self-Assessment Questions Taking the Initiative and Value Addition

1. What do you understand by "initiative?" Explain with examples in your own words
2. What do you understand by "value addition" and its importance?
3. How does it help in your workplace? Explain with examples.
4. Give five synonyms from the cluster of initiative.
5. Enumerate five things that you can do to take the initiative
6. Enumerate five points/things that you can do for value addition.
7. How can you be proactive? How does it help in your productivity and performance in the workplace?
8. How did Facebook start? What, according to you, are reasons for its success?
9. What are the three main reasons, according to you, for the success of BYJU'S?
10. What is the biggest contribution of Elon Musk to the world, and how did he become so big?
11. Write about the Google story in about 250 words.
12. What do you understand from the following Quotes?

We don't get a chance to do that many things, and everyone should be really excellent. Because, this is our life.

—Steve Jobs

Don't be afraid to tread new ground, but do a sanity test.

—Sabeer Bhatia

We now accept the fact that learning is a lifelong process of keeping abreast of change. And the most pressing task is to teach people how to learn.

—Peter Drucker

13. What do you feel were the three main reasons for the spectacular success of NIIT?
14. How did Symbiosis start? What is the single reason for its success?
15. Who started Stanford University? What are the contributions of its alumni?
16. How did Amul start and how did it become so successful?
17. What is the reason for the spectacular success of Wipro? How did Azim Premji change the organization to take it to great heights?
18. Write the Honda story in your own words—around 250 words? What is the most important lesson you learned from the Honda story?
19. What is IISc famous for? What is at the heart of its core competence?
20. How did BITS Pilani start and where has it reached today? Write in about 200 words.
21. Research a successful business model in agri-business in India and write about it in 250 words.

9788196261856